WEDDING DAYS

Norma Simon

Pictures by Christa Kieffer

Albert Whitman & Company, Niles, Illinois

 *For my husband, Ed, with love.*

Library of Congress Cataloging-in-Publication Data

Simon, Norma.
    Wedding days/Norma Simon: illustrated by Christa Kieffer.
       p. cm.
Summary: Discusses the decision to marry, wedding plans, the wedding itself, second marriages and the formation of new families, and anniversaries.
   ISBN 0-8075-8703-6
   1. Weddings—United States—Juvenile literature. 2. Marriage service—United States—Juvenile literature. 3. Marriage customs and rites—United States—Juvenile literature. [1. Weddings. 2. Marriage customs and rites.] I. Kieffer, Christa, ill. II. Title.
HQ745.S55 1988
392'.5'0973—dc19   87-28957

Text © 1988 by Norma Simon
Illustrations © 1988 by Christa Kieffer
Design by Gordon Stromberg
Published in 1988 by Albert Whitman & Company
Published simultaneously in Canada by General Publishing, Limited, Toronto
All rights reserved. Printed in the United States of America.
10 9 8 7 6 5 4 3 2 1

A wedding is the beginning of a marriage, the beginning of happy days.

A man and a woman marry
when they love each other
and decide to spend their lives together.
Before Aunt Jean and Uncle Mike got married,
they bicycled and went to movies together.

They ate dinner together.
They read together, walked together,
and talked and talked and talked.
They found out they were
very special to each other.

One day Aunt Jean told her family,
"Mike and I love each other. We want to get married."
Everyone was excited and happy.
Jean's family met Mike's family,
and wedding plans were made.
Jean and Mike decided
when their wedding would be,
where they would get married,
whom they would invite,
what invitations to send,
what clothes they would wear,
what food to serve,
what music to play,
and what flowers Aunt Jean would carry.
They chose their wedding rings.

Aunt Jean and Mike asked Kathy to be their flower girl.
They asked Jeremy to carry their rings.

On a sunny day in June,
Jean and Mike were married.
The bride's family and friends wore fancy clothes.
The groom's family and friends were all dressed up, too.

The bridesmaids, the ushers, and Mike
walked in time with the music.
Kathy tossed pink flower petals from a pretty basket.
Jeremy carried gold rings on a velvet pillow.
The organist played
"Here comes the bride, all dressed in white"
as Aunt Jean and her father walked down the aisle.
(Aunt Jean's mother cried a little.)

The bride felt very beautiful,
and the groom felt very handsome.
Everyone listened to the words of the wedding promises.
They heard Jean say, "I do."
They heard Mike say, "I do."
Jean and Mike slipped the gold rings on each other's fingers.
The minister said,
"I now pronounce you man and wife."
Mike and Jean kissed,
and the church was filled with smiles.

After the ceremony, there was a wonderful party.
The guests shook hands, hugged, and kissed.
They held up their glasses
and toasted the bride and groom.
Everyone ate and ate. Everyone danced and danced!
A photographer took lots of pictures.
The bride and groom cut the tall white cake.
When Aunt Jean threw her wedding bouquet,
Aunt Amy caught it.
That meant Aunt Amy was supposed to marry next.

At the end of the party,
Jeremy and Kathy and all the guests
threw rice at the bride and groom
while they drove away.
On their car was a sign: JUST MARRIED!
Kathy could read the big letters
all the way down the road.

Mike was now *Uncle* Mike.
He was part of Kathy's family.

After two people are married, the man becomes a husband and the woman becomes a wife.

They live together, and they share their lives.
Maybe they will move into a new house or apartment.
They buy groceries together and wash dishes together.

They sleep together.
They work to pay their bills.
Their friends and families come to visit.

They try hard to love and care for each other
in happy times,
in sad times,
when they are healthy,
and when they are sick.

Maybe they will have children to love, too.
Husbands become fathers and wives become mothers when children are born or adopted.

Sometimes married people are very unhappy together.
They decide to be divorced.
If they marry another time,
they hope it will be forever.

When Mandy's mother married Steve,
it was a second wedding for both of them.
Mandy came to the wedding, and so did Steve's children.
Mandy's mother sewed her own pink wedding dress
and made blue dresses for Mandy and for Steve's daughters.
The wedding was fun for the bride and groom
and for all their children.

After Mandy's mother and Steve were married,
their children became stepbrothers and stepsisters.
Steve was Mandy's stepfather, and Mandy's mother
was a stepmother to Steve's children.

People marry in many different places—
in a church,
in a synagogue,
in a house,
in City Hall,
outdoors in a garden.

or beside the sea.

Farmers,
bus drivers,
cowboys,
librarians,
plumbers,
actresses,
dentists,
secretaries,
carpenters,
teachers,
firefighters,
lawyers,
young people,
old people —
all decide to marry.

In every country in the world,
there are brides and grooms and wedding days.

A wedding is so special
that people save souvenirs—
their wedding invitations,
wedding napkins decorated with silver bells,
the tiny bride and groom that sit on top of the cake,
and lots and lots of photos.

Sometimes a bride wears the same wedding dress her mother and grandmother wore.
Then she puts it away for her daughter to wear someday.

When a couple has been married one year,
they celebrate their first anniversary.
Every year there is another anniversary.
After twenty-five years it's called a *silver* anniversary.
After fifty years it's called a *golden* anniversary!
There are special parties for such special days.

Do you know the day when your
mother and father
have their anniversary?
Do you know the day when your
grandpa and grandma got married?
Grandparents like to show you pictures
of their wedding and the weddings
of everyone in the family.

For grandpas and grandmas,
mothers and fathers,
brothers and sisters,
children and stepchildren,
aunts and uncles and cousins,
friends,
but most of all for brides and grooms,
wedding days are happy days.